COMMITTEE.

President,

WILLIAM BLUNDELL, Esq., Crosby Hall.

Vice-Presidents,

JAMES BRANCKER, Esq.,

W. W. CURRIE, Esq.,

WILLIAM EARLE, Jun., Esq.,

JOSEPH C. EWART, Esq.,

A. HEYWOOD, Esq.,

LAWRENCE HEYWORTH, Esq.,

WILLIAM RATHBONE, Esq.,

Colonel GEORGE WILLIAMS,

WILLIAM WINSTANLEY, Esq. M.D.

Treasurer,

Mr. WILLIAM THORNHILL.

Solicitor,

Mr. P. F. CURRY.

Bankers,

Messrs. SAMUEL HOPE & CO.

Secretary,

Mr. JOHN S. RADCLIFF.

Mr. JAMES AIKIN,

Mr. GODFREY BARNSLEY,

Mr. THOMAS BLACKBURN,

Mr. THOMAS COGLAN,

Mr. W. P. FREME,

Mr. C. GRIMSHAW,

Mr. SAMUEL HOPE,

Mr. GEORGE HOLT,

Mr. S. T. HOBSON,

Mr. JOHN HASELDEN,

Mr. VINCENT HIGGINS,

Mr. WILLIAM JACKSON,

Mr. TIMOTHY JEVONS,

Mr. ROBERT JOHNSON, Jun.,

Mr. JOSEPH KING,

Mr. PATRICK LEONARD,

Mr. JAMES MULLENEUX,

Mr. WM. ROBERT PRESTON,

Mr. GEORGE QUAYLE,

Mr. GEORGE ROBINSON,

Mr. JAMES RYLEY, Jun.,

Mr. RICHARD SHEIL,

Mr. WILLIAM SANTLEY,

Mr. WILLIAM SLATER,

Mr. THOMAS URQUHART,

Mr. JOHN WYBERGH,

Mr. R. W. WOOD,

Mr. WILLIAM WALTHEW,

Mr. WILLIAM WOOD,

Subscriptions or Donations to the Funds of the Association will be received by the Members of the General Committee or District Committees; by the SECRETARY, at the *Liverpool Reform Association Office, Orrell-place,* 74, *Lord-street,* (for the present,) between the Hours of Twelve and Two each day; or at the Office of Mr. P. F. CURRY, Solicitor, Orrell-place, Lord-street.

LIVERPOOL

REFORM ASSOCIATION.

———

AT A NUMEROUS MEETING OF REFORMERS, HELD
AT THE CLARENDON ROOMS, ON THURSDAY, THE 5TH
OF FEBRUARY, 1835,

It was Resolved,

That an Association, to be called "THE LIVERPOOL
REFORM ASSOCIATION," be immediately formed,
and that the following, as its Objects and its Rules, be
adopted:—

OBJECTS.

1st.—To promote the cause of General and Local Reform
by all legal means.

2d.—To superintend the Registration of Electors for the Borough of Liverpool, and also that of the County Electors who Poll in the Liverpool District, with the view of getting the names of all those inserted who are legally qualified, and of objecting to the Registration of those who do not possess the necessary qualification.

3d.—To prevent, counteract, and expose all attempts to intimidate or corrupt the Electors.

RULES.

1st.—The Association shall consist of all those Friends of Reform who have already signed their names in the Book provided for the purpose, and have subscribed not less than *Ten Shillings annually.* All persons hereafter wishing to become Members shall be proposed and seconded by two Members of the Association, and subscribe at least Ten Shillings per annum. The Subscription to be payable immediately for the current year, and to be considered due on the first of January in each succeeding year.

2d.—A Committee of Twenty-one Members, with a President, Vice-Presidents, and a Treasurer, shall be annually chosen by the Members of the Association; the said Committee to have power to add to their number, to fill up any vacancies that may occur, to appoint a paid Secretary, and to procure whatever legal assistance may be necessary for carrying into effect the objects of the Association. Five of the Committee to form a quorum.

3d.—The Committee shall make arrangements for the establishment of District Committees, who shall be empowered to receive Subscriptions (for promoting the objects of the Association) of any sum, though less than Ten Shillings per annum. The amount of such Subscriptions shall be paid at stated periods to the Treasurer of the Association.

The Subscribers shall have the right of sending two Deputies from each District to the General Meeting.

All Acts, Rules, and Regulations of the District Committees shall be submitted to the consideration of the General Committee, and no part of the proceedings of any District Committee shall be considered finally arranged and settled until it has been reported to, and received the sanction of, the General Committee.

4th.—The ANNUAL MEETING of the Association, for the Election of Officers, and for general purposes, shall be called the first week in January.

A GENERAL MEETING shall be held the first week in June in each year, and at such other times as the Committee may see fit; and also whenever called on to do so by a Requisition, addressed to the President or Secretary, and signed by Ten Members.

TO THE ELECTORS.

————

THE possession of a vote in the Election of our Representatives in Parliament is a high privilege, granted to the individual (in trust) not only for his own advantage, but also for the benefit of the community at large, and especially for the great mass of his fellow subjects, whose circumstances in life do not enable them to obtain the Elective Franchise.

It depends entirely on the proper exercise of this important duty whether we have a good and cheap, or a corrupt and extravagant Government.

It is therefore unquestionably the duty of every man, who has it in his power, to qualify himself to vote for such persons to represent him in Parliament as may (in his opinion) seem best fitted to obtain for the whole people the inestimable blessings of a *good, economical,* and *impartial* Government; and he who neglects to qualify himself, or refrains from the exercise of this invaluable privilege (if he possesses it), or votes contrary to the conscientious dictates of his unbiassed judgment, from any motive whatever, inflicts an injury on the community, and betrays the sacred trust reposed in him by his country.

The Reform Association deeply laments that, on many occasions, the acts of those from whom (considering their station in society) a different line of conduct might have been expected, have rendered strong measures of protection to the Electors, and exposure of the intimidators, absolutely necessary.

The Association will therefore use its utmost efforts to protect the Voter in the free exercise of his important privilege, and will use all legal means to expose and punish those who basely attempt to intimidate the Elector from the honest and fearless discharge of his duty to the community.

The Association hopes to shew that such individuals are powerful only in inflicting injuries on their friends, and that they will ultimately find themselves obliged to abandon all attempts to exercise dishonest influence.

The Association begs to call the attention of the Electors to the annexed Abstract from the Reform Act, which points out the qualification necessary to constitute a County or Borough Elector, and the mode of getting Registered.

JOHN S. RADCLIFF,

Secretary.

By the Reform Act, the qualifications of a County and Borough Elector, and the mode of getting Registered, are as follows :—

COUNTY.

If Lands or Tenements (not being within the Borough) are held at a yearly rent of £50, bare occupation as Tenant from year to year is sufficient, and it is immaterial by what tenure they are held.

Also the occupation of Lands or Tenements of the yearly value of £50, as Sub-Lessee or Assignee of any under Lease of a term originally created of not less than 20 years, and it is immaterial how small a portion of the term may remain unexpired.

Also the original Lessee of a term originally created for 20 years of the yearly value of £50, or the Assignee of such term, is entitled to Vote, and in this case also it is immaterial how small a portion of the term remains unexpired, nor is occupation required.

So also the occupation of Lands of the yearly value of £10 as Sub-Lessee or Assignee of any under Lease of a term not less than 60 years, and it is immaterial also in this case how small a portion of interest in the term remains unexpired.

Also the original Lessee or the Assignee of such a term of the Lands of the yearly value of £10.

In this latter case occupation is not required, nor is tenure material in any of the above cases, but Twelve months' possession previously to the last day of July is required in all.

Also being seized of an Estate for life or lives of the yearly value of £10.

A Freehold Estate in Lands or Tenements of the annual value of 40s. is sufficient to give a Vote in the four following cases:

1st.—If it be an Estate of Inheritance.

2d.—If it be not an Estate of Inheritance, but only an Estate for life or lives, if the Elector was seized previously to the 7th of June, 1832, the day on which the Reform Act received the Royal Assent, and continues so seized at the time of Registration and of Voting.

3d.—If acquired subsequently to that day, if the Elector be in actual and *bona fide* occupation at the time of Registration and of Voting.

4th.—Or if acquired subsequently to that day, if it came to the Elector by Marriage or Marriage Settlement.

A Mortgagee, Trustee, or Executor, if *in actual possession, and receipt of the rents,* or the Mortgagor, notwithstanding such Mortgage, may claim to be Registered and Vote.

BOROUGH.

The right of those who claim to Vote (independent of Freemen) in the Borough is given to every person who shall occupy, either as Owner or Tenant, any House, Warehouse, Counting-house, Shop, or other Buildings being either separately or jointly with any Land occupied therewith, by him as owner or occupier therewith, by him as Tenant under the same Landlord, of the clear yearly value of £10, and who shall have been rated in respect of such Premises, to all rates for the Relief of the Poor.

N.B.—All the Poor Rates and Assessed Taxes must be paid before the 20th of July, as well as the Shilling for Registration.

If the Property be *jointly* occupied, and the clear yearly value be of such an amount that, when divided by the number of occupiers, shall give a sum of not less than £10 to each, every occupier can claim to be Registered and Vote.

Any Person whose Name shall have been omitted from the Overseer's List may claim to have his Name inserted, by giving notice in writing, on or before the 25th of August, to the Overseer.

On or before the last day of July in every year, the Overseers are bound to make out a List of all Persons entitled to Vote, and are bound to keep true copies, which may be perused by any Person, *without payment of any fee*, at all reasonable hours, during the two first weeks after the Lists are made.

Any Persons who are actually on the Register, or who

claim to be put on any List, may object to the Name of any Person, but Notice must be given before the 25th of August, to the Overseer and to the Person to whom they object.

Any further information or assistance in getting Electors duly Registered, and forms of the different Notices, Claims, &c., may be had at the Office of the "Reform Association," Orrell Place, Lord-street, between the Hours of Twelve and Two o'Clock each day.

D. Marples & Co., Printers, Liverpool.